New Year's Day

Lynn
Peppas

Crabtree Publishing Company

www.crabtreebooks.com

Crabtree Publishing Company
www.crabtreebooks.com

Author: Lynn Peppas
Coordinating editor: Chester Fisher
Series editor: Susan LaBella
Editor: Adrianna Morganelli
Proofreader: Molly Aloian
Editorial director: Kathy Middleton
Production coordinator: Katherine Berti
Prepress technician: Katherine Berti
Project manager: Kumar Kunal (Q2AMEDIA)
Art direction: Rahul Dhiman (Q2AMEDIA)
Cover design: Shruti Aggarwal (Q2AMEDIA)
Design: Cheena Yadav (Q2AMEDIA)
Photo research: Dimple Bhorwa (Q2AMEDIA)

Photographs:
AP Photos: p. 22; Mark Lennihan: p. 6
Art Directors: PhotoStock Israel: p. 21
Corbis: Bernard Annebicque: p. 11; Bettmann: p. 8; Yang Liu: p. 18
Dreamstime: Ashley Whitworth: p. 1, 10
Getty Images: Feng Li: p. 19
IndiaPicture: p. 30
Istockphoto: Julie Fairman: p. 26; Karen Hogan: cover, p. 5;
      Dirk Richter: p. 14; Jenny Swanson: p. 4
Mary Evans Picture Library: p. 27
Photolibrary: Alex Mares-Manton: p. 7; Visual Impact: p. 24
Reuters: Mike Segar: p. 29; Eric Thayer: p. 28
Rex Features: Lester Ali: p. 31; Tommy Holl: p. 23
Shutterstock: cover, folio image, p. 25; ; Arvind Balaraman: p. 13;
      Kzenon: p. 12; Lowe Llaguno: p. 17; Howard Sandler: p. 20;
      Ekaterina Vysokova: p. 15; Jerry Zitterman: p. 16
Stockxpert: Sedmak: p. 9

Library and Archives Canada Cataloguing in Publication

Peppas, Lynn
      New Year's day / Lynn Peppas.

(Celebrations in my world)
Includes index.
ISBN 978-0-7787-4762-8 (bound).--ISBN 978-0-7787-4780-2 (pbk.)

      1. New Year--Juvenile literature. I. Title. II. Series:
Celebrations in my world

GT4905.P46 2009   j394.2614   C2009-905187-7

Library of Congress Cataloging-in-Publication Data

Peppas, Lynn.
      New Year's day / Lynn Peppas.
            p. cm. -- (Celebrations in my world)
      Includes index.
      ISBN 978-0-7787-4780-2 (pbk. : alk. paper) -- ISBN 978-0-7787-4762-8
(reinforced library binding : alk. paper)
      1. New Year--Juvenile literature. I. Title. II. Series.

GT4905.P462 2010
394.2614--dc22
                                                                                      2009034810

Crabtree Publishing Company
Printed in China/122009/CT20090915

www.crabtreebooks.com   1-800-387-7650

Published in Canada
Crabtree Publishing
616 Welland Ave.
St. Catharines, ON
L2M 5V6

Published in the United States
Crabtree Publishing
350 Fifth Ave.
59th floor
New York, NY 10118

Published in the United Kingdom
Crabtree Publishing
Maritime House
Basin Road North, Hove
BN41 1WR

Published in Australia
Crabtree Publishing
386 Mt. Alexander Rd.
Ascot Vale (Melbourne)
VIC 3032

Contents

What is New Year's Day? **4**

New Year's Eve **6**

An Old Holiday **8**

Fireworks **10**

Resolutions **12**

New Year's Foods **14**

Parades **16**

Chinese New Year **18**

Rosh Hashanah **20**

New Year's Music **22**

Other New Year's Customs **24**

New Year's Symbols **26**

New Year's at Times Square **28**

New Year's Around the World **30**

Glossary and Index **32**

What is New Year's Day?

New Year's Day is a holiday that almost everybody celebrates. It falls on the first day of a brand new year. Most people celebrate it on January 1.

Midnight is the start of New Year's Day.

4

People of some **cultures** go by different **calendars** and celebrate New Year's Day on a different date.

New Year's Day is a public holiday. Most people do not go to work or school. Many plan parties or dinners with friends and family.

- Friends like to get together for parties on New Year's Day.

DID YOU KNOW?

New Year's Day starts at midnight, or 12 a.m., and lasts until midnight that day.

New Year's Eve

People start to celebrate New Year's Day the night before. Cities around the world have special New Year's Eve celebrations. Many have concerts that lead up to midnight.

Some cities hold outdoor New Year's parties.

DID YOU KNOW?

Many people stay awake until midnight to welcome the New Year in as soon as it begins. Have you ever stayed up that late?

6

People have a good time while they wait for the New Year to come.

When it is 10 seconds before midnight, people start counting down: 10–9–8–7–6–5–4–3–2–1. When midnight comes they shout, "Happy New Year!" People kiss and hug at New Year's.

At midnight, people wish each other a "Happy New Year!"

An Old Holiday

People have been celebrating a new year for over 5,000 years. Long ago, there were no calendars. People relied on nature to tell when it was the end of a year.

- Long ago, Romans believed that their god, Janus, could look backward and forward.

Some people believed the New Year came in spring. Others thought the end of the year was in the fall.

Ancient Romans began their new year on January 1 over 2,000 years ago. Their god Janus had two faces. People believed that he looked back on the old year, and forward to the new one.

• Ancient Roman leader, Julius Caesar, was the first person to make New Year's Day on January 1.

DID YOU KNOW?

Roman leader, Julius Caesar, called the month January after Janus, the two-faced god.

9

Fireworks

Many cultures celebrate New Year's Day with fireworks. Fireworks were first made in China about one thousand years ago.

People believed fireworks scared away bad luck with the loud noise they made.

- Fireworks are a good way to welcome in a new year!

DID YOU KNOW?

The New Year's Day firework display held in Madeira, Portugal, in 2006, was the largest one ever. More than 60,000 fireworks were lit!

People used them to ring in the new year so they would have good luck only.

Large cities such as Niagara Falls, Canada, hold fireworks displays at midnight on New Year's Eve. Fireworks have different patterns and colors. Some look like colored flowers or spiders in the air.

These men are making fireworks.

Resolutions

On New Year's Day, many people think about the past year. Some people want to make the coming year even better. Many people make resolutions on New Year's Day. A resolution is a promise you make to yourself to change something in your life.

These people are working on a resolution to get in shape.

Young people might make resolutions to try harder at school, or to be nicer to their families, pets, or friends. Some try to keep their rooms clean. Another resolution might be to use less energy and help Earth.

People write down their list of resolutions so they do not forget them.

DID YOU KNOW?

One popular resolution that many people, both young and old, make is to get fit in the new year.

New Year's Foods

Some people around the world think that what you eat on New Year's can bring you good luck in the year to come. Cabbage is believed to make you richer. Some think that cabbage leaves look like paper money.

Pork sausages and sauerkraut (pickled cabbage) are lucky foods to eat at New Year's.

Pork is lucky, too, and many eat it with their cabbage to give them extra luck.

What about a lucky dessert? Try rice pudding with an almond in it. People from Norway eat this at New Year's.

These black-eyed peas will soon be cooked and eaten.

DID YOU KNOW?

Some people in the United States eat black-eyed peas on New Year's Day. They believe it will bring them good luck in the New Year.

Parades

Parades on New Year's Day are held around the world. In the U.S., there are some famous ones. In Philadelphia, there's the New Year's Day Mummers' Parade. Mummers are actors.

Mummers are costumed actors who welcome in the new year.

DID YOU KNOW?

The Rose Bowl is a college football game first played after the New Year's parade in 1902. This game is called the "Granddaddy of Them All."

New Year's clubs plan all year for the parade. This **tradition** began over 100 years ago.

The Tournament of Roses parade in Pasadena, California, is over 100 years old. It is held each year on New Year's Day. Floats with flowers parade down the street. Millions of people watch the parade on television.

Floats are decorated with flowers for the annual Tournament of Roses parade.

Chinese New Year

The Chinese New Year's celebration falls on different dates between January 21 and February 20. Many Chinese people celebrate in their homeland of China. Other Chinese communities celebrate it wherever they live. It lasts for 15 days but most people today celebrate for two days.

• Good luck and money come in red envelopes during the Chinese New Year.

DID YOU KNOW?

Some children get red envelopes with money gifts inside for Chinese New Year. The gift brings good luck for the person who gets it.

In Vancouver, Canada, everybody loves to watch the annual Chinese New Year parade. People enjoy the lion dance teams. A group of people makes a long cloth lion. Dancers make the lion move underneath the cloth by moving poles. The lion is thought to scare away any bad luck in the new year.

People underneath lion and dragon puppets make them come to life in Chinese New Year parades.

Rosh Hashanah

Rosh Hashanah marks the beginning of a new year for Jewish people.

It falls on different dates every year between September 5 and October 5. Rosh Hashanah begins at **sunset**.

- A shofar is blown during **synagogue** services at Rosh Hashanah.

DID YOU KNOW?

At Rosh Hashanah, people blow a horn called a shofar. These horns are made from animal horns such as a male sheep called a ram.

On Rosh Hashanah, many people go to a synagogue. It is a holy place to worship God. They ask God to forgive anything wrong they might have done in the past year.

People eat apples dipped in honey on Rosh Hashanah. They believe that eating this will bring a sweet new year.

- Apples dipped in honey will bring sweetness in the new year.

21

New Year's Music

The most popular song to ring in a new year is *Auld Lang Syne*. The words are from a poem written in 1788 by Scottish poet, Robert Burns. The words were set to an old folk song.

• Famous Canadian bandleader, Guy Lombardo, made *Auld Lang Syne* a popular song for New Year's.

DID YOU KNOW?

The rock band, U2, wrote a popular song called New Year's Day. It became a hit single in 1983. People still listen to it around the world today.

A Canadian musician named Guy Lombardo used the song for New Year's in 1929. Today, it is used in celebrations throughout North America and Europe.

Bono, from the band U2, sings the popular song, *New Year's Day*, at concerts all year round.

23

Other New Year's Customs

Many people believe that what you do on New Year's Day will be carried on for the rest of the year. This is why they follow a **custom** of spending time with people they like.

Sharing a tasty meal with the people you like best is a good way to start off a new year.

Many people think that the first person to visit a house on New Year's Day will bring luck into the house. A young man brings the best luck. This person is called a first-footer, or the first one to put a foot in the house.

It is lucky to have a young man step inside your house first at New Year's.

DID YOU KNOW?

Some people believe that wearing new clothing and shoes on New Year's Day will bring them riches.

New Year's Symbols

A baby is a **symbol** for the new year. Babies stand for a new beginning. Sometimes the baby wears a top hat, and **banner** with the new year on it.

Many places in North America give special gifts to the first-born baby in the new year.

Baby New Year grows up to become an old man named Father Time. He passes his duties on to the next Baby New Year.

An old man named Father Time is a symbol of the year that has passed. He carries an hourglass to help him mark time. He sometimes wears a banner with the old year on it.

- Father Time shows the old year has passed. A baby stands for a new year.

DID YOU KNOW?

Fireworks, party horns, church bells, and banging pots and pans are some of the noisier symbols used at New Year's.

27

New Year's at Times Square

For over 100 years, Times Square in New York City, U.S., has been a favorite place to be on New Year's Eve. Here, one million people wait for the new year to come.

You can watch the New Year's celebration at Times Square on T.V. or you can visit in person.

DID YOU KNOW?

The Times Square ball is made of glass and electric lights. It weighs over 11,000 pounds (5,000 kg) and is 12 feet (3.7 m) from one side to the other.

Many more people from around the world watch this event on T.V.

At one minute before midnight, a giant sparkling New Year's Eve ball slowly makes its way down 77 feet (23 meters) on special cables in just one minute. When it gets to the bottom it is the new year.

The Times Square ball slowly makes its way down to welcome in a new year!

29

New Year's Around the World

In India, some **Hindu** people celebrate New Year's in the spring. People wear yellow clothes and decorate their houses with flowers. Others celebrate it in the fall during another festival called Diwali.

In every different language, people wish each other a "Happy New Year."

During Diwali, families honor their beliefs by praying.

Many people of different cultures like to clean house before the new year comes so everything will stay in order for the year ahead. You should not clean on New Year's Day though because you might sweep away your good luck.

These brave people take a dip in icy water on New Year's Day.

DID YOU KNOW?

Some groups of people jump in icy waters on New Year's Day. These cold dips are thought to keep their minds clear throughout the new year.

31

Glossary

ancient Thousands of years old

banner A strip of cloth bearing a title or name that is worn as a piece of clothing or hung up as a sign

calendar A chart that shows the days, weeks, and months in one year

culture A group of peoples' beliefs, habits, and customs

custom The way things are done by a group of people for many years

Hindu A person who believes in the religion of Hinduism

sunset The time of day just before evening, when the sun goes down in the sky

symbol Something that stands for something else

synagogue The holy place where Jewish people worship God

tradition Customs or beliefs that are handed down from one generation to another

Index

ancient Romans 8, 9

Auld Lang Syne 22

Caesar, Julius 9

Canada 11, 19

China 10, 18

custom 24, 25

food 14, 15

Janus 8, 9

Lombardo, Guy 22, 23

midnight 4, 5, 6, 7, 11, 29

Mummers parade 16

Portugal 10

public holiday 5

puppet 19

resolution 12, 13

Rose Bowl 16

synagogue 20, 21

Times Square 28, 29

U2 22, 23